WINDRUSH

Contents

Written by Clive Gifford

6 9341 300173518

The West Indies

The West Indies is a group of islands between the Caribbean Sea and the western Atlantic Ocean. Many of the islands have high mountains, thick forests and sandy beaches. Bigger islands, such as Jamaica, have busy towns and cities, too.

Kingston is Jamaica's capital city.

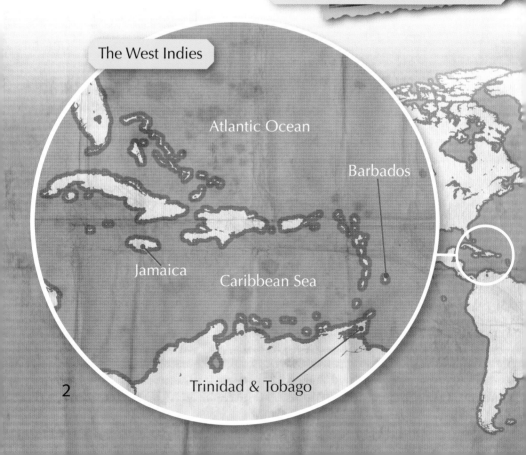

The West Indies

Atlantic Ocean

Barbados

Jamaica

Caribbean Sea

Trinidad & Tobago

The islands are tropical, which means that they have warm sunshine all year round, and crops such as bananas, ginger and **sugar cane** can grow.

In the 1940s, part of the West Indies, including Jamaica, Barbados, and Trinidad and Tobago, was ruled by Britain. Many people on these islands grew up thinking of Britain as a kind of second home. This was because they spoke English, read British books at school, and heard British news on the radio.

bananas growing on a farm in the West Indies

3

Island life

Today, the warm **climate** and beautiful scenery attract tourists to the West Indies. But in the 1940s, most people who lived in the West Indies were farmers and life could be hard. Sometimes, poor harvests meant that the farmers didn't get enough money for their crops, and there wasn't always enough work.

harvesting crops in the West Indies

Children often grew up in big families, surrounded by aunts, uncles, grandparents and cousins. They may not have had much, but they were free to play on the beaches and in the rivers and fields around their homes. Schools were strict and teachers were treated with respect. Children often left school to work on the land with their parents, as there were few other **opportunities** for them.

a classroom in Jamaica

A new opportunity

Some West Indians wanted to get a better education and learn new skills. Many dreamt of a better future and were prepared to travel to make it happen.

From 1948, the UK government allowed people living in places that it ruled, including the West Indies, to move to Britain. Many West Indians thought that there would be lots of new opportunities for them in Britain. Others wanted to go for the adventure.

In May 1948, a passenger ship called the *Empire Windrush* was sailing to Jamaica on its way to Britain.

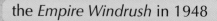
the *Empire Windrush* in 1948

A month before it arrived, 300 places on board were advertised. The fare was just over £28 for a one-way ticket.

For many families, this was a lot of money. At the time, most people in the West Indies earned £3 to £6 a week. There wasn't enough time to save up, so people sold things they owned, or borrowed money, to buy a ticket.

PASSENGER FILE

Sam King was 22. He'd worked as an engineer in the **Royal Air Force** in Britain and was eager to return. His family sold three cows to pay for his fare.

Come to Britain
Passenger Opportunity on the Troopship
Empire Windrush
Sailing about 23rd May
Fares: Cabin Class £48
Troop Deck £28

Leaving home

On 24 May 1948, the *Empire Windrush* left Kingston harbour in Jamaica. Hundreds of people waved their loved ones goodbye.

All 300 tickets had been sold, but more people wanted to travel. An extra 192 passengers were taken on. There were no cabins for them, so they stayed in the open air on the deck.

Most passengers were young men, as there were more jobs for men than women at the time. There were just five families on board. A few people who really wanted to go, but couldn't afford tickets, hid on the ship and travelled as **stowaways**.

PASSENGER FILE

Vince Reid was 13 and was the youngest passenger on board. He'd never left his island home before and was excited to be going on a great adventure.

Hopes and plans

The passengers had different hopes and plans.
Some wanted to stay in Britain for a year or two.
Others hoped to remain for a lot longer. Some planned
to send for their families if life in Britain went well.

This map shows the route taken by
the *Empire Windrush* on its journey
from the West Indies to Britain.

UK

Bermuda

Cuba

Atlantic Ocean

Mexico

Jamaica

The passengers were looking for many different kinds of jobs. Some were trained mechanics, builders, welders or woodworkers, looking for skilled jobs on building sites and in factories. Others were tailors, musicians, accountants and students.

It took almost a month for the *Empire Windrush* to reach Britain. Many tried to enjoy the trip as much as possible. Groups of passengers formed bands and sang. Others read books and played card games and dominoes.

Arrival

The *Empire Windrush* arrived in Britain on 22 June 1948. People quickly went their different ways. Some had families in Britain. Others had jobs to go to. Some people rejoined the Army or Air Force units that they'd served in during **World War II.**

12

There were 230 people who needed somewhere to stay. The British government arranged for them to be taken to south London. There, they stayed in an underground shelter that people had used a few years before to hide from bombs in the war.

Their first meal in the shelter was a typical British dinner of roast beef with all the trimmings and **suet pudding**, served by the **Women's Voluntary Service.**

Finding work

There were lots of jobs that needed to be done in Britain, and most of the passengers quickly found work. More than 70 started working in factories. Others found jobs with bus and tram companies, and some went to work in hospitals as nurses and health workers.

Some people got jobs as bus conductors, selling tickets.

There were also a lot of building sites in London, as war-damaged parts of the city were being rebuilt. Some of the plumbers and welders who'd travelled on the ship found jobs on these sites.

Skilled workers, like welders who knew how to join metal, helped to rebuild British cities.

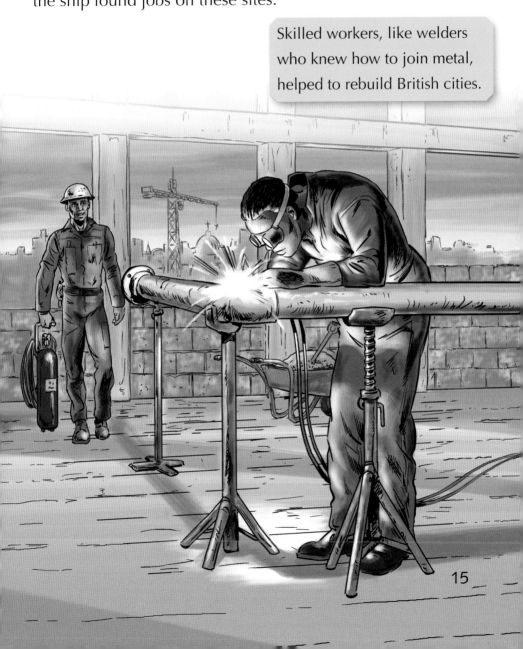

Daily struggles

The jobs that some of the *Empire Windrush* passengers found weren't the kind of work that they'd hoped for, but to start new lives in Britain, they had to take what they could get. Some people couldn't get jobs that they were trained for, such as welding, engineering or nursing, and had to take unskilled jobs as cleaners and labourers instead.

This was hard, because unskilled jobs were low paid and didn't offer many chances for **promotion**. Some passengers found this very disappointing as they'd expected more opportunities in Britain.

British factories offered different kinds of jobs from the ones that people had done in the West Indies. This woman is making shoes.

Life in a new country

Life for the new arrivals wasn't easy at first. People missed their families and friends. Others found the cold, wet weather hard to deal with and longed for the warmth of home.

Some people lived in very cramped conditions.

Others didn't like British food. Supplies of some everyday foods, such as meat, butter and sugar, were limited after the war, and were still being rationed in 1948. This meant that people could only buy small amounts of them each week.

Many of the foods that were common in the West Indies, such as **yams**, **saltfish**, bananas and other tropical fruits, were hard to find anywhere in Britain.

An adult would have lived on this set of rations for one week.

19

Being in Britain

Life in Britain wasn't what many of the *Empire Windrush* passengers had expected. War had destroyed parts of many big cities and, although the country was recovering, some people still lived in **poverty**.

Most British people were white. Many of them knew very little about the West Indies, and most had never met a black person before. Some British people were friendly to the new arrivals, but many others were not, and there was often an unpleasant attitude towards them.

Many parts of London were in ruins after the war.

Far from friendly

Most passengers on the *Empire Windrush* had expected to feel welcome in Britain. But some British people were rude and unkind to them because they looked and sounded different.

British landlords often refused to rent rooms to black people and had signs that said, "No blacks" on their doors and windows.

Many of the *Empire Windrush* passengers were turned away from some shops and cafés, and were sometimes shouted at in the streets. **Racist** slogans were painted on walls near where they lived.

"K.B.W." stood for Keep Britain White.

A home in Britain

Although some of the *Empire Windrush* passengers returned to the West Indies after a few years, many others stayed and raised their families in Britain.

★
PASSENGER FILE

Aldwyn Roberts, under his stage name, Lord Kitchener, became a popular singer in clubs in London in the 1950s and made several records. He returned to Trinidad in 1962.

25

Remembering *Windrush*

The arrival of the *Empire Windrush* was only a small news story in 1948. Today, it is thought of as an important point in history. This is because it was one of the first ships to carry large numbers of West Indians to Britain. By 1962, around 180,000 people from the Caribbean had travelled to Britain on other ships.

Today, around 600,000 West Indians live in Britain and work in many different jobs including business, medicine, education, sport and music.

This model of the *Empire Windrush* was used in the opening ceremony of the London Olympics in 2012.

Glossary

climate	the typical weather conditions in a certain place
opportunities	chances to do something
poverty	extremely poor living conditions
promotion	being given a higher level of job with more responsibility and higher pay
racist	unfair and unkind attitudes about race
Royal Air Force	the flying section of the British armed forces
saltfish	a traditional West Indian dish of dried, salted fish
stowaways	people who hide on a ship to travel without paying the fare
suet pudding	a heavy steamed sweet sponge
sugar cane	a tropical plant grown for the sugar it produces in its stem
Women's Voluntary Service	an organisation set up during World War II to provide shelter, protection, food, first aid and clothing to people in need
World War II	a war that took place between 1939 and 1945 across many parts of the world
yams	tropical vegetables similar to sweet potatoes

Index

Life in the West Indies

tropical climate

strict schools and fewer opportunities

poor harvests and not enough work

space to play

Life in Britain

jobs with bus and tram
companies and in hospitals

unskilled jobs as cleaners
and labourers

unkind and racist attitudes

cold, wet weather

31

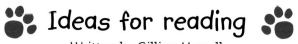

Ideas for reading

Written by Gillian Howell
Primary Literacy Consultant

Reading objectives:
- predict what might happen on the basis of what has been read so far
- discuss the sequence of events in books and how items of information are related
- draw on what they already know
- continue to apply phonic knowledge and skills as the route to decode words
- explain and discuss their understanding of books that they read for themselves
- make inferences on the basis of what is being said and done

Spoken language objectives:
- maintain attention and participate actively in collaborative conversations
- give well-structured descriptions, explanations and narratives for different purposes, including for expressing feelings
- articulate and justify answers, arguments and opinions
- participate in discussions, presentations and debates

Curriculum links: Geography; History

Interest words: Caribbean, climate, scenery, opportunities, government, mechanics, builders, plumbers

Word count: 1,440

Resources: pens, paper, internet

Build a context for reading

- Read the title together and look at the cover photograph. Ask the children what impression the photograph gives them. Ask what they think the book might be about and why they think this.

- Turn to the back cover and read the blurb together. Ensure the children understand that West Indians come from the West Indies. Ask the children to say what opportunities means. Ask them to suggest why this event was important.

- Read the list of contents together. Ask the children to say if this book needs to be read in sequence and why.

Understand and apply reading strategies

- Look together at the map on pp2–3 and locate the West Indies and Britain. Discuss what the children know about the West Indies.

- Ask the children to read the book using a quiet voice. Remind the children to use their knowledge of phonics and contextual clues to work out words they are unsure of.